Smart Icon Sticke

A Practice Aid for Self-motivated S

T0085313

By Joy J. Song

※ Many of these icon stickers are explained in *Secrets to Scales Series* (Hal Leonard. 2013) written by Joy Song.

 **Korea Institute of Piano Pedagogy**

KIPP's mission is to spread good music through effortless teaching and fun learning, based on the words "You will know the truth, and the truth will set you free." (John 8:32)

www.kipp.or.kr

KIPP's website contains a variety of useful information, such as Dr. Song's video lectures, seminars and lessons, publications and a directory of studios and teachers teaching Dr. Song's method.

Dr. Joy J. Song

A native of South Korea, Dr. Joy J. Song is regarded as an innovator in the field of piano pedagogy whose publications of educational piano materials and psychology books on personality types are widely acclaimed. *Sonatine Secrets* was introduced at MTAC 2013 by Hal Leonard and was praised as an innovative, fun and effective way for students to study essential repertoire. *American Music Teachers* (Feb./Mar. 2014) described the book as providing first-rate musical concepts for younger students with a method utilizing fun, computer-style icons. *9 Gifts for Pianists*, another steady-selling textbook, has been employed in piano pedagogy classes for a long time.

Dr. Song started the piano at age five and received BM, MFA and DMA (ABD) in Piano Performance and DMA in Piano Pedagogy. She has also studied the fields of Early Childhood Development, Music Education and Coaching.

Smart Icon Sticker Book
A Practice Aid for Self-motivated Students

Published by	KIPP(Korea Institute of Piano Pedagogy), Distributed by Hal Leonard
Address	7777 West Bluemound Road, Milwaukee, Wisconsin 53213
Phone	414-774-3630
Fax	414-774-3259
Web site	www.halleonard.com

Publisher	Joy J. Song
Cover Design	Marina Lee
Illustration	Jung-Yeon Choi
Design	Young-Ran Kwon
English Translator	Yoon-Jee Kim

Published	Jun 2014

UPC 8-88680-02498-7
ISBN 978-1-4803-9836-8
Item Number HL00131378

 Korea Institute of Piano Pedagogy

Korea Institute of Piano Pedagogy
www.kipp.or.kr

Smart Icon Stickers for Posture

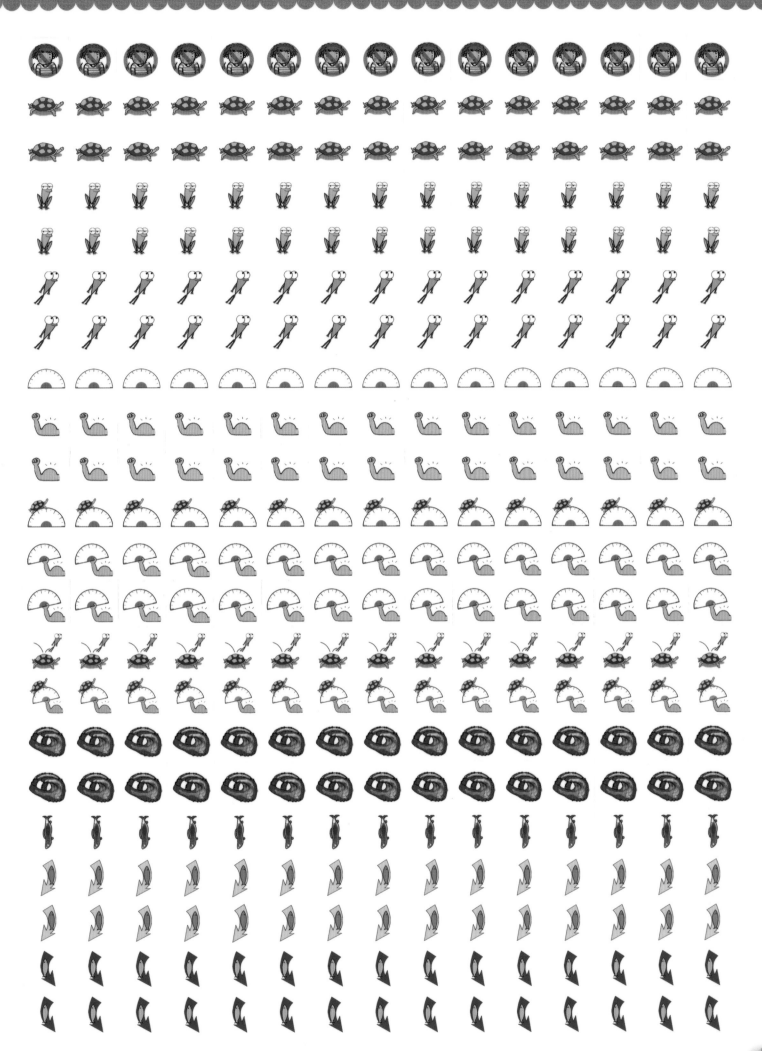

Who am I?

Find me in the Stickers pages and explain what I do.

put a matching sticker	Icon Name	Explanation
SAMPLE	The Protractor	Aligned with the keyboard

Smart Icon Stickers for Posture

Legend

Welcome to the Icon Village!

ICONS for Posture

Icon	Explanation	Suggested Use
Shoulder down	Whenever those sneaky shoulders go up without you knowing it, bring them down with this smart icon sticker.	Ecossaise (L. v. Beethoven) (Allegro)
The Turtle Shell	Palm like a turtle Fingertips like hammers	Minuet (J. S. Bach)
	Prepare with a lowered wrist. Leap to make sound resonant.	Ecossaise (L. v. Beethoven) (Allegro)
	Wrist jumps like on a pogo stick.	

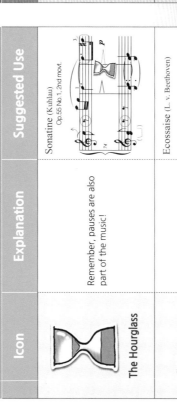

ICONS for Musical Interpretation

Icon	Explanation	Suggested Use
The Hourglass	Remember, pauses are also part of the music!	Sonatine (Kuhlau) Op.55 No.1, 2nd movt.
The Supple Wrist	The wrist moves diligently and delicately to adjust its position according to the movement of each finger.	Ecossaise (L. v. Beethoven) (Allegro)
After - sound	After-sound guy will help you to sound more musical.	Sonatina (M. Clementi) Op.36 No.3, 1st movt. Spiritoso
	After-sound and Before-sound will create beautiful bridges	legato

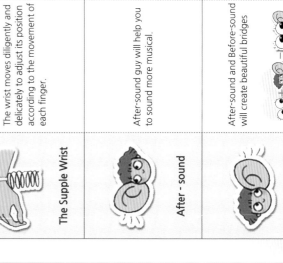

Harmonic ICONS for Expression

Icon	Explanation
Dissonant	Pearl is uncomfortable because of a dissonant harmony.
Not resolved	Pearl is dissatisfied because something hasn't resolved yet.
Transition harmony	No final resolution took place, but Pearl is still a bit relieved.
	Pearl is completely satisfied after having reached the goal.

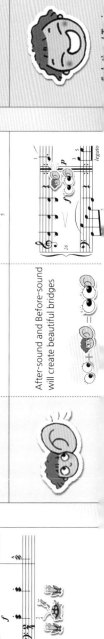

Icon	Description	Music Example
Minor / Sad	Pearl is touched and has tears in her eyes.	
sf (sforzando)	Pearl is trying to make an important point.	

Suggested Use

Sonatina (M. Clementi) Op.36 No.3, 1st movt.

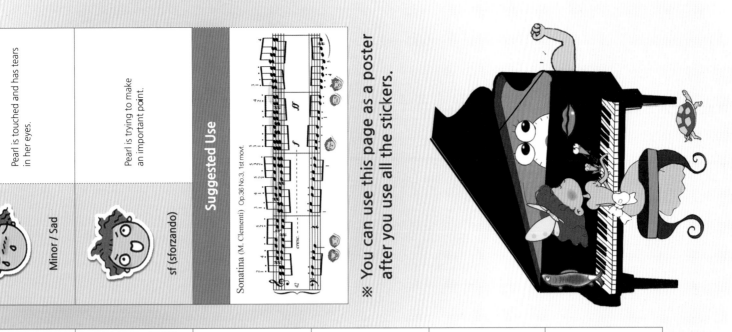

※ You can use this page as a poster after you use all the stickers.

Icon	Description	Music Example
Ms. Preview	Ms. Preview prevents mistakes. She may be the hardest worker of the Icon village!	Impromptu (F. Schubert) Op.90 No.3 — Moderato
The Quiet Feather	A feather descends very slowly and lightly. For anything from p to pp, imagine a feather coming down!	A Short Story (H. Lichner) — p espressivo
The Butterfly	Whenever you have to use the wrist more, feel free and flutter like a butterfly.	Sonatine (Kuhlau) Op.55 No.1, 2nd movt.
Sticky	You know how it feels when you step on a gum? It feels wonderfully sticky.	Minuet (J. S. Bach)
The U-Turn	Does a car speed up when making a u-turn? No, it has to slow down. Decreasing speed means soft playing, just as a car driving upwards and downwards will have to speed down and up.	Minuet (J. S. Bach)
Melody Line	Bring out the outer lines (soprano and bass) clearly, and let the inner lines (alto and tenor) fill the space inside softly.	Sonatina (M. Clementi) Op.36 No.3, 1st movt.

Icon	Description	Music Example
The Protractor	Wrist needs to move	Minuet (J. S. Bach)
The Bicep	This muscle must appear every time the thumb or the pinky must play.	Ecossaise (L. v. Beethoven) (Allegro)
The Baseball Glove	Move your fingers from the palm. Imagine moving your fingers in a baseball glove!	Minuet (J. S. Bach)
The Standing Thumb	The thumb is like a living fish. / with a firm muscle.	Minuet (J. S. Bach)
The Turning Fish	Right thumb: The right thumb to the right. Left thumb: The left thumb to the left.	Happy Farmer (R. Schumann)

※ All of the information on this legend has originally come from *Sonatine Secrets* by Joy J. Song

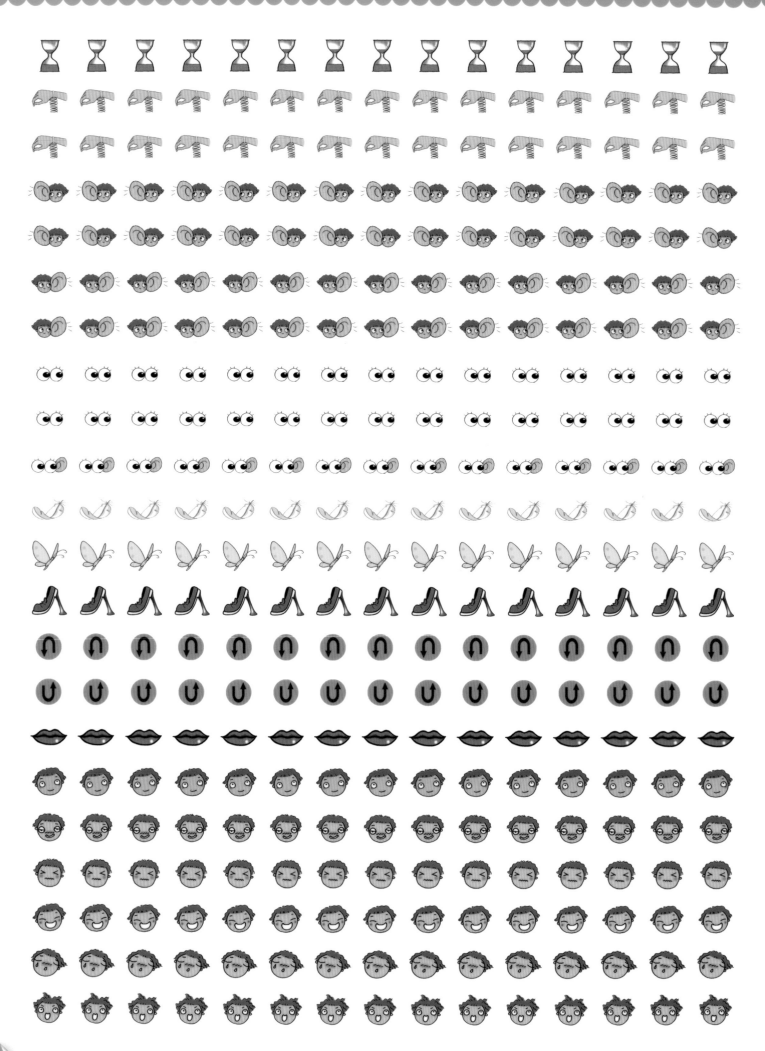

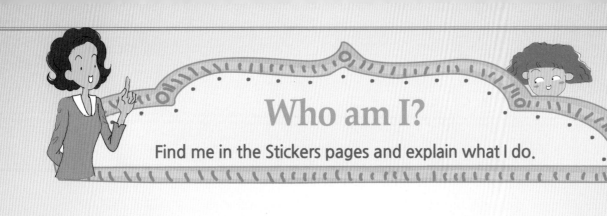

Who am I?

Find me in the Stickers pages and explain what I do.

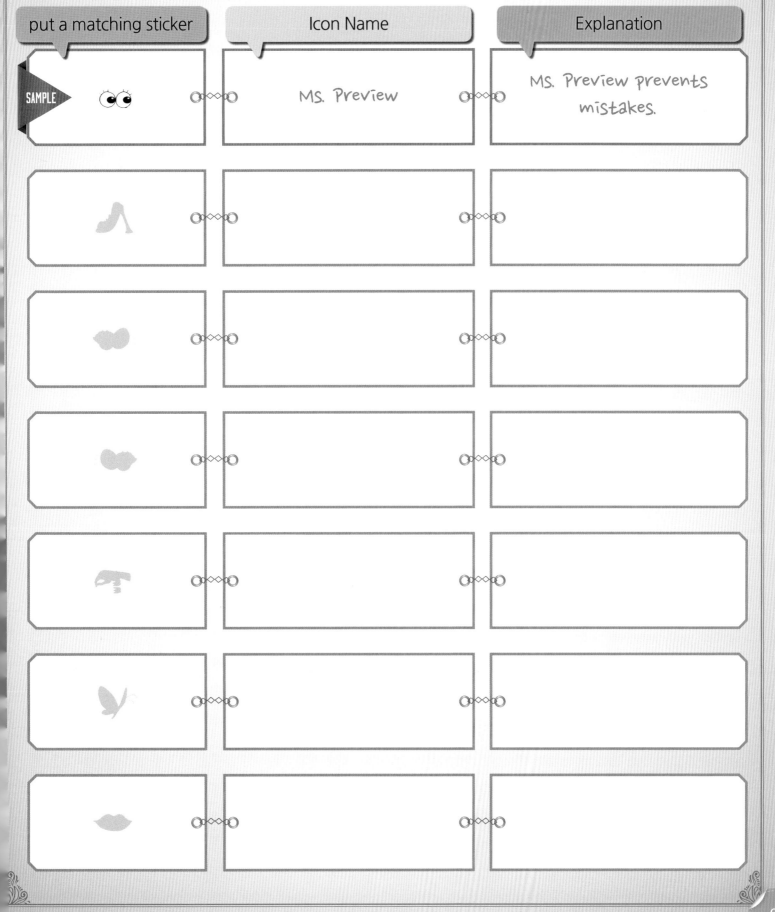

put a matching sticker	Icon Name	Explanation
SAMPLE	MS. Preview	MS. Preview prevents mistakes.

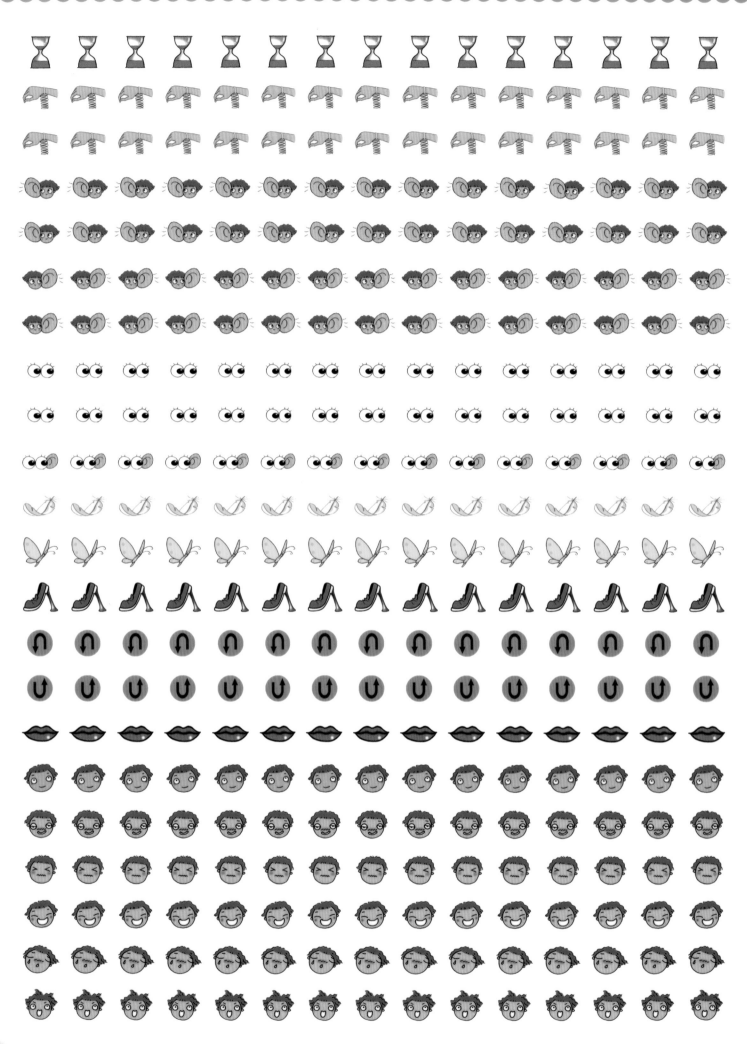

Arirang

Korean Traditional

Twinkle Twinkle Little Star

English Lullaby / French Melody

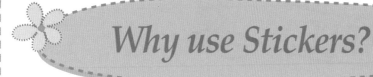

Why use Stickers?

🌸 A weary teacher's plea for help

After an entire day of talking during lessons, a piano teacher is inevitably worn out and does not want to utter another word for the rest of the day. I myself once had to have a throat surgery because of all the talking I had done over 30 years of teaching 40 hours a week.

Talking is of course something we can hardly do without. But having to say the same things over and over like a parrot is a torture for everyone.

> "Left hand softer! Shoulders down! Don't let your fingers collapse! Bounce the wrist!
> Firm fingertips and flexible wrists! Find the right balance between the hands!
> Always look ahead! Align the arms to the keyboard! Voicing!
> Sing with your pinky! More melancholy! Connect the sounds! Legato, legato!"

The list goes on and on, and the teacher is weary. What about the students? Unfortunately, they don't listen anymore because these same instructions are old news for them. This way of teaching becomes something of a nagging, and soon, they don't even want to learn the piano anymore.
The problem of repetitive oral instructions is a mutual one for both teachers and students.

🌸 Transforming an absent-minded student into a self-motivated one

Is there a way to avoid this ordeal and to scrap talking from teaching altogether? Also, how wonderful would it be if students could have an artistic goal in mind, listen internally, gain awareness for their own problems and fix these out of their own will? The Smart Icon Stickers were born out of these wishes. As I used these stickers over the years, I have discovered that there was no need for me to explain verbally anymore. As soon as I began placing an icon sticker, students instantly changed what they were doing. An hour-glass sticker made them wait, and a preview sticker encouraged them to look ahead. Even better: the after-sound sticker opened up their closed ears, and as a result legato-playing happened naturally. When I noticed these changes, I asked my students to place stickers wherever they saw fit before each lesson; this way, they began learning how to interpret on their own.

> Self-motivated pianists: these were precisely the kind of students I had dreamed of cultivating.
>
> Icon stickers proved to me that an effective communication can be wordless; after all,
> isn't music also a form of wordless communication? If we can communicate to our students in
> the easiest, the most fun way, aren't we able to achieve an ideal pedagogical model?

The Smart Icon Stickers were originally a part of *Sonatine Secrets: A Creative Approach to Developing Technique and Musicality* (distributed by Hal Leonard). It is an immense pleasure for me to see the sticker book also made available separately. This ingenious teaching aid has been a refreshing guide to young and older students alike, and it will continue to inspire passion toward interpretation and performance of anything from Sonatine to pieces by Mozart, Beethoven, Chopin, Brahms and others.

2014 in Beverly Hills,
Joy J. Song